That Strapless Bra in Heaven

Poems by

Sarah Sarai

© 2019 Sarah Sarai. All rights reserved.
This material may not be reproduced in any form, published,
reprinted, recorded, performed, broadcast,
rewritten or redistributed without
the explicit permission of Sarah Sarai.
All such actions are strictly prohibited by law.

Cover design by Shay Culligan

ISBN: 978-1-950462-20-9

Kelsay Books Inc.
kelsaybooks.com
502 S 1040 E, A119
American Fork, Utah 84003

*& I wish the god of this place
would come down from the roof & wake
me herself.*
  Meg Day

       *After
the afterlife there's an afterlife. A stand of
cottonwood trees getting ready all over again*
  Carl Phillips

Wouldn't it be enough to be just fat or just old and dying?
  Ellen Bass

Contents

Wish Me Luck	9
Hatred Is a Death Threat	10
What an Arroyo Can Do	11
Corpses and Cats	12
The Short Lapse of It	14
The Reversible Lobotomy of Confusion	15
Longing for a Blue Sky	16
Science and Change	17
Hockney at Bellevue	18
Popularity	19
Backward Fables	20
This Way and That	21
After the Greeks Tippy-toed Out of a Horse	23
Tippi as Pippi	24
So Let's See if I Have this Right	26
This Once-in-a-Lifetime Opportunity	28
Who punched the banana!	30
Family	31
Embalming	32
White People Are on my Mind These Days	33
Anxieties	34
Motherhood	35
Thank the Cashier	36
After the Plague Years	37
Six Aunts Wobbling	38
One Day a Year You Can Take Something	39
Home from the Met	39
On the Shelving Cart	40
Marilyn Hacker	42
True Grit	43
Love Being Among Them	44
Like Wings	46

You Are the Confusing Identity I Write For	47
By Any	48
Blame It on Family	49
The Quiet Softness	50
It Was the Year the Birds Held a Conference	51
Keeping It Holy	52
No One Asks	53
Early Jazz	54
Drink, Child	55
Not Simple Is Joy nor Cosmology	56
A Scarlet Moss	58
And the Ships Set Off	59
Please Don't Think I'm Being Disrespectful	60
Time Lives to Thwart Chronology	61
Saint Beauty	63
Call Me Sheena	64
Inquisition	65
So Tender Beauty	66
An Interrogatory	67
The Risen Barbie	68
White Tunnel and the Night Return	69
From Love, Imagination	71
Far on the Lake, Watery Lake	72

Notes
Acknowledgments
About the Author

Wish Me Luck

I replaced phone to cradle,
knowing it was just
something to say,

that luck's more than
preparation meeting opportunity
wooing a congressman
saving up for a sex change.

It's not hard fact in collaboration
with ambiguity,

not briefs longing for
the strapless bra up in heaven.
It's a result,

what Jesse Pinkman
told Hank Schrader.
Mr. White's so damn lucky.

Which may not bear out
when the machine gun's
fired its last, or may,
because fulfillment is in the
eye of the storm.

Could be luck's the
River Jordan of fiction,
a passage, part of the daily miracle,
a Glad bag of coal
Superman will squeeze
into diamonds.

I saw him do it.

Hatred Is a Death Threat

Siri's rich aunt am I.
Clap twice and I'll start the coffee or
make the girl get it done.

A model home of the future am I,
a dream acquisition,
the bungalow they sold you on wanting.

Resistance is an educated guess,
a straw breaking backs of caravan-
owners but not owners of caravan-owners.
Please, not the camels.

Hatred is a death threat,
not an imperative.
A consequence,
        not an inevitability.

We who shed tears clap
twice and twice more for
the light to shine itself
in the unnavigable dead end.

If there is a way out,
tell me, Siri. Or join me.
Tarnish the obelisk. Admit of
the body, don't resist it.
        And do start the coffee.

What an Arroyo Can Do

It is possible for an arroyo to hold water,
just as a gutter, one of its definitions, can.
But mine is high in the desert and dry as scorn.
The sun bakes long-suffering into that dirt.
That's what an arroyo is, a gully of dirt
the color of old pottery and scrub,
like a god scattered a burden of
wild straw and told it to dig deep into
the color of acceptance. Make roots.
"Start a family."

"This is home," the wild straw said as it clung
to the land. Not at first.

But after so many cycles of skies talking
blue streaks to nights. Then
the scrub made friends. Fell in love.

I was drinking when I fell into an arroyo.
Scrub raked my hands like a rancher
if he thought I was after his daughter.
Unless he hoped for a daughter-in-law.
A piñon tree ordered the scrub to resist my pull.
"Stay grounded!"

You know—when we think stars are trembling?
It's the constellations laughing.
I saw them. I was on my back.
The stones, which I haven't even introduced,
snarled at dirt and scrub to ignore me.
No one argues with stones.

Corpses and Cats

During the Siege of Leningrad
Citizens ate corpses and cats.

Beneath the Hermitage
Framers ate glue.

Old women walked passageways
Dark and molding to protect treasures.

What does 'old' mean except
A man doesn't want to fuck you.

Big deal. The Musical Comedy
Theatre did not shutter.

A grand actress thawed make-up
Over a lamp. It had to go on.

After one of *The Three Musketeers*
Dropped dead onstage

She tried to speak her lines
But couldn't, for grief.

The Luftwaffe bombed Soviet
Planes, idle on the tarmac.

Stalin was a coward-leader
Like Trump and also a fool

Who trusted Hitler and ruled from
his dacha while Mother R. starved.

Who knows quite what to say
about that onion deep-fried

in snow. I don't. Except its people
ate cats and corpses and lived.

The Short Lapse of It

A bad night of it
Coleridge in paradise
Shelley in an antique land
apparitions unable to convey
the difference of it

hackle-raising drifting through it
a midnight scrutineer
a brutal fly-by by the stars
unveiling this night flight not
easy until released

into the short lapse of it
the wilds of its hunky dory
no colder than a month of
the deniable terror of it
the night-think falling for

the Valhalla of it
the Vegas of it
the pick a or b of it.
why so panicked, dream,
the bad conscience of it?

The Reversible Lobotomy of Confusion

Her life, a proper noun till
the improper ones.
The gay bar where.
The dyke pool hall when.
That demand for balance
way before anyone cares.
Astronomical oppositions ravaging
her astronomical chart.
Yup/Nope Her/He
Half-empty/and Emptier.
Ping-ponged, sling shot,
she is a wars-of-the-universe re-enactor.
The rock, hard place.
That suburban desert between.
She pities not-knowers in crinoline
nervous to be near, to be
her. Fearful of association's challenge.
Enter the lesser halves.
The husbands swished-shoe
appalled by strength and shamed by
wealth, they. Mere re-enactor,
she didn't write the script she revises.
Articles of a sound constitution
see her into middle age as strong
in her belief we are all cross-dressing.

Longing for a Blue Sky

I am goal-oriented like an orgasm,
exhausted already by details of your ego.
My details are colored "hesitation" and "confidence?"
though age, she educates.

My mood is London longing for a blue sky.
I take the Hudson River as my lover,
the Southwest as my comforter,
Mount Shasta as my tomb.
Who wouldn't want to spend millennia
in a fine female breast?

In my pain—everything I need to be pleased.
I am pleased already, could you shut up!
See me, in a woman's burial mound?
Your ego destroys nothing. Not even itself.

Science and Change

I declined a knighthood honoring my heroic efforts at keeping heroism effortless, something I perfected while lateral-to-prone-ish and modeling a languid nobility which defined my Why Not Give It A Shot-ness much as when a road I am on forks, and what with poor decision-making, which leads to backtracks and do-overs, I try-out all tines of the many—dessert—dinner—terrapin—toasting—tea—spork—to name six—and fret I am mistress of not much in the long run, short haul, or myself, let alone the silver which needs a polish. A whack and a polish. So end-of-day I slide between sheets to digest myself, me, a caterpillar who believes in science and change.

Hockney at Bellevue

There's all kinds of ways to
enter one of

Hockney's pools, to
part the cerulean acrylic,

become California,
no longer dream young men

in radiant absence but
engage perfections of skin

and promise of
love eternal's blank comfort,

including this way, in winter
3,000 miles away and

over a sludge of feta and
fries,

indistinct life's landscape
not thrilled with

its inability to be simply
necessary (without

a pallid cuisine of industrial
vistas, no inside, no

hospital, no chance to see
humanity restored by

experts reconstructing
pools of human flesh).

Popularity

Snakes are pretty damn famous.
More than they deserve to be.
I've slithered on sand,
Snapped my fangs at an ankle,
Soaked sun, rock-snoozed.
I dig the desert.
Have I told you that?
How much I dig the desert?
Low desert, high desert, any desert.
Name a desert. Sahara?
Dig it. Name another one.
Gobi? Good choice! Mojave?
Been there, done it, hankering to do it again.
Also, I'm a very spiritual person.
Another life I was a prophet.
Prophets. Deserts. Hello?
How spiritual is a snake?
Can a snake hiss like an angel?
I can. Hisssssssssssss.
Screw you for doubting me.
I should be more famous than a stupid snake.

Backward Fables

Internalize a single-cell flame
of butterfly blowback.

What's to lose?
Clear of this beat—abounding sod,
and—to pine for—apricot musk,
a dandelion-scatter.

The ovule-into-seed sails on
breezes obliging elevation and release.

I am made linear to say,
make the span plausible.
Step over and out,
set store by process, not monolith.

The sod, its wobbly dandelion,
the nervous daffodil field
line the way.

And now a quick tale of caution.
"No straight road, issuing from it."
[John Ashbery] ["Meaningful Love"]

Those backward fables?
What if Lot's wife and Eurydice
honor the contract?
Boundaries are propaganda.

This Way and That

> *It was a fairy funeral.*
>   William Blake

On the garden bed of
Blake's fairy procession
roll this and that, these ways
of midnight pleasure

in enchantment and
commonplace wisdom
like don't touch the fairies,
they're sensitive.

Act within a soul
populated by
sightings and wistful affection,

see the filmstrip is at
high-enough speed
life's fluidity's felt,
as at the funeral Blake saw,

a bodylet laid out on a leaf.
Authentication enough for me,
that fairies exist, I e-mailed you
who reminded me
Blake saw God when he was

four. God got down on Her
omni-aching knees
now and then to spy on
William Blake
and could hardly contain Her

infinite self, waiting for
the artist to become Heaven and
those paintings to be flashed to
the good and bad alike as proof of

the great mystery of vision
even She can't figure out.

After the Greeks Tippy-toed Out of a Horse

Arms, and the man…
        Virgil

Christ almighty was that a year.
The damn war FINALLY over
though the many-faced hero heroed-on
ten more to slay a weaver's suitors lined-up
and slicked-back on Ithaca Ave.

THAT year, warriors de-warriorized, or tried to.
Mothers had died fathers had died wives
husbands aunts uncles sisters and brothers had died.

But not a golden-guy,
with eyes a glinty glint
and sweaty sweat on biceps bulging.

Sailing sea-y seas Aeneas ashored on
land of a lady founder
who took one gandy gander and
plunged into bicepboy's eyes—not deep pools—

and after the jumping-off-joy—
no small joy we agree—was deady dead,
having lit sticks and self and such when
loverboy sailed again. Soon,
the city-on-a-boot he birthed,

Rome, all Latinated and lawyered up,
warriorized and empired, though,
we admit, the engineering was good.

Those aqueducts and bridges, those walls.
They were something else.

Tippi as Pippi

Listen. See that?
Cleanliness is next to Godliness,
the blonde on the right,
in the chair? No,
Godliness isn't a blonde,
Cleanliness is.
Cleanliness is the blonde,
her hair in a French roll.
You'd think Alfred Hitchcock
would've cast
Cleanliness in
The Birds but he went with
Tippi Hedron
who could've been
Pippi Longstocking,
I can see it, Tippi as Pippi,
given my given
which I now give you,
that all things are being equal.
Tippi knew of Pippi,
who doesn't,
yet Pippi knew not Tippi.
Cleanliness
doesn't spread gossip.
Like every other schmuck,
Godliness wants to see a movie,
but not with Cleanliness
cause of the buttered popcorn
issue, the issue of
buttered popcorn being
little baby grease slicks,
(not little Grace Slick
who dropped acid
when she was pregnant).

You've never heard of
Jefferson Airplane?
And yet the world spins,
one pill making us
smaller at a time,
Cleanliness helpless
over the mess,
Godliness, feet up,
a Sprite in the cup holder,
snorting at coming attractions.

So Let's See if I Have this Right

> ...*that savage forest*...
>   Dante

You're not dead you're middle-aged
and slogging through forests dense as

a king's woods stocked with golden-
needled pines and swift hart but you're

not anywhere and don't know where
anywhere is. A shade is

summoned for the three-day tour,
maybe Melville, charting to the sandy

bottom of the nature of God.
Or Emily, enlivening eternity.

It takes time, whatever
that is, to meet the messengers.

To understand your grief is felt by
the living and loved by the dead.

Now and ever sleek, a greyhound bounds
after a wolf, so no one must face reality,

the wolf being original fear made external,
reality requiring original anesthesia.

So there you are, creeped out and eager
and your guide gets ominous and

warny—you're headed for a wild ride.
What you should say is *Pinch me*.

Or read the wrapper and pinch yourself.
You're asleep. We all are. Get used to it.

Do something. Like the dishes.
And don't forget to pay the rent.

This Once-in-a-Lifetime Opportunity

Once a coworker disappeared, on
vacation, I imagined, imagining

his folks, San Francisco, Chinatown,
the Mission District, hills. We'd

compared San Franciscos with mine
being the Haight, and fuchsias in

Golden Gate Park where they bloom
like it's a once-in-a-lifetime opportunity,

this plunging into life to be loved.
Later I wondered about moons

rocking his eyes and who'd dusted his
face with chalk, cut out a silhouette of

him, breathed half-life in it so he was
a shaky doily, a minor dimension of someone

I once knew, inhaling and suffering.
One morning he pulled me aside to

advise I never check myself into Bellevue.
I was Assistant Web Producer

learning HTML, how to code if you
wanted only one word bolded,

not paragraph or page. We linked to
a webcam on Times Square. I was asked

to seed the forum and created a flash-
of-a-girl in blue, and parents who

hoped they spotted "our Felicity"
on 43rd Street. When my boss asked

if I was Felicity and family I lied.
I wondered about the pajamaed at Bellevue.

"The world doesn't make sense. Go away."
As for advice, generally I say, "Shut up,

already," though a make-up artist friend
advised me on lip-liner, took me to Duane

Reade to buy a stick matching a shade of
lipstick a graphic designer at Estee Lauder

gave me, a fuchsia, as from my west of
aching beauty. What a nice thing to do.

Who punched the banana!

If Euclid you would.
Back off, pal, that's Jacob's well.
What *did* Jesus do?
Three angels visited their dealer from grad school.
On top of Old Smokey, again?
Looked it up.
Not over it yet.
What would *Mary* do?
Something is as it seems.
You may hit the next man who says,
"I don't understand why any woman voted for Trump."
The last man who said it was blind.
Wear an orange vest when in human nature.
Too much is as it seems.

Family

My three siblings are older than I am.
The biggest Russian doll who
contains we younger is Jean,
and it is with her I saw the movie *Jaws*.

For *The Exorcist* I just went along with
a loose assemblage, friends of friends.
That's what you do with movies,
you see them, though it's opening
day and you are blithe as a donut on
an oblong tray at Winchell's.
If the Vatican set up a table in
the theater lobby like Seventh Day
Adventists in the subways I'd have
signed up for a catechism class on
the spot. That was some scary shit.

One time Jean sent me a clipping from
the San Francisco Examiner.
Two sisters, 76 and 82ish, lived together
on Nob Hill until the older murdered
the younger. *Watch your back, kid,*
Jean printed in the margin.

I knew *Jaws* was going to be epic,
am unsurprised by this future of
plastic predators-of-the-seas rising from
bubble baths on *Saturday Night Live*.
But when the shark leapt from an
endless ocean of lost whalers, Jean
and me, we screamed, we shrieked,
we grabbed each other's hands.

Before and after *Jaws* I have known terror.
That was the only time I ever held my sister's hand.

Embalming

It even had a name: "Freddy."
The Washington Post, July 17, 2016

I finally get to share good news.
The stolen brain was not
my brain which has a stem
connector to my tree of life.
It was a medical-school brain,
also good news as this bit of
real life is creepy but not
Hannibal Lector creepy.
It makes sense that a thief
would get high smoking weed
and embalming fluid and
a stolen human brain.
There is order in our world.
Although the thief's mother
expressed surprise at finding
a brain under her porch.
If my torso weren't attached
I don't know where my head
would be. I hope not under
a porch next to a stolen brain
or alongside a heart beating
desperately at planks above.

White People Are on my Mind These Days

We are going to disappear.
I say good riddance though
I'll miss myself.

Robert said, Well what culture do they have.
The next day my answer.
Er, the novels of Thomas Hardy,
farmers bent by winds off the Channel?

Do the dying move on with grace,
knowing there's new life and they're part of it
no matter?
Some hit the dirt oblivious to
lights strung up in the tunnel.
This is personal but what isn't.

Explorers were curious gold.
Conquistadors filed teeth for blood.
I can't figure out history.

I said we were on the way out and Robert's
Robert said, Don't worry,
we'll cause more damage
before we're gone.

My great-nephew promised to be kind,
as he looked into my eyes and
spotted the loving goddess,
clawing to get out.

Anxieties

*...and the sun came out of the dark sky to show
the Wicked Witch surrounded by a crowd of monkeys...*
                                        L. Frank Baum

What do monkeys worry about,
their imaginations grown dim?

They can shoot fires at our doubt.
What do monkeys worry about?

Their flying wings always so broad
to fright us limb to limb.

What do monkeys worry about:
Our imaginations grown dim?

Motherhood

I'm talking Satan,
who fathers Rosemary's
baby in a so-so apartment
in The Dakota.
But in The Dakota is
no such thing as so-so
so strike that.
East across Central Park
West, leaves tremble at
a gloom of shadows
lurching behind shades
a disturbing pale, pale
as Rosemary's well-off
New York neighbors
who could be pool-
side with Mr. and
Mrs. Robinson except
mere materialism is
merely a brass ring
too accessible to reach
and still care. Reach
and still care. Minnie
boils a chocolate
pudding for Rosemary
and her generically named
husband, Guy. Oh!
The banality of evil.
Rosemary wants a kid,
gets a kid, and suckles
that ravenous babe.

Thank the Cashier

Etiquette must, if it is to be of more than trifling use, include ethics as well as manners.
                                        Emily Post

Easy enough to thank the cashier so I do.
I am rather fabulous,
you may have noticed, well-bred,
not flaunty of assets.
Crass is not a word you'll use
to describe me, not behind
my back nor in front of it.

I dip my fat red
strawberry toes in the sweat
of the cashier's brow
as if it were fondue.
You don't? Let's forgo guilt.

If you ask me, someone got it
wrong or was mistranslated by
some arriviste scholar
with holes in her socks.

The poor may be around
but are not always with us.
They can't afford the rent.
My place, like zeroes in
an equation, must be held
like my hand by someone
at the club as I weather
heartache and storm
in my brother's yacht.

If he has sailed to the islands
his heated gazebo must do.

After the Plague Years

Narrow waist, soft rise
of a dimple, hips like
river banks sweet grass and
marsh, chiseled ivory dusted.
She sighs into her bed,
eager for the feel of
her husband's clever muscles,
a home she's always known,
for that catch in his eye as if
memory were sinister.
His foot cracks a bowl
the slave neglected.
Cursing, Oedipus
encircles Jocasta's heat.
Torches are dark.
Something is at the door.

Six Aunts Wobbling

Slim Aunt Shirley went
home and straight Aunt Gin
wiped her furred lip's
beer moustache,
something I sport now and
then but not her bosoms.

Queer Aunt Denise,
who is not Denise my
dyke-aunt, summoned
the spirit of my aunt passed over—
Tilly with the bad eye.
She was a whip at cards.

Poppy yodels
before and after shots.

Aunt Denise who is my
dyke-aunt partnered with
Queer Aunt Denise.
She has the Tilly-gift at cards.

Poppy and bosomy Gin crossed
ankles like fingers as they
cheated and lied
in the way of families.

Both Denises shouted at Poppy.
Stop yodeling, you!
She poured another round.

One Day a Year You Can Take Something Home from the Met

You have to have been born one block from
the Long Island Sound.
The museum's insurance company requires proof
Louie's was serving clam chowder that night.
Your parents' bed would have had
to be, of course, your first mattress
and when you think back,
sixty years later, it is essential
you wonder, Where the hell
were my sisters?
Two crones and a gypsy
must tell of three fires burning in
black heaven, and a pack of
physicians are to dip nibs
in blood and sign-off on
Connecticut's faint-hearted
swooning. This is tricky.
Fridays, in Connecticut, a swoon
is hard to distinguish from a pass out.
Vodka goes down real easy
across the Sound.

On the Shelving Cart

"Pictorial Archive of Female Touch"
"Freud's How-To: Volume IX
    of the Academy of Futile Investigations"
"Library of Geological Curiosity: Female Orgasm
    Challenges to the Richter Scale"
"Proceedings of the Society for Sensual Revelation"
"Darwinian Arguments for the Quick Grab"
"Theoretical Orgasm: A Position Paper"
"Real Deal Orgasm: Authentications"
"Paradigms of Necessary Ecstasy"
"Tendencies to Colonize the Cunt"
"No Longer that Rare Rapture:
    An Expository Essay"
"Inner Thigh Love in the Early Middle Ages"
"Your Porous Skin So Hungry"
"Mechanical Schemata for Quickies"
"Rounded Hip on Rounded Hip:
    A Cartographer's Dream"
"Universal Primer on Teaching Touch"
"Finger-probing Vaginal Regions and
    Other Investigatory Bliss"
"Stately Pleasure Domes"
"Love's Globalization: Sacred Texts on
    Orgasm as Universal Verity"
"Venture Capitalism: Artifact of
    Nothing in Contrast to Women Sighing"
"American Medical Association's
    Acknowledgement of the Embodied
    Ache for Pleasure"
"The Atlas of Female and Non-binary
    Explorations in a New World"

"American Medical Association
        Addendum: Immeasurable
        Possibilities of Gratification"
"I Married a Vagina: An Inside Story"
"Big: America Awakens"
"Expansionists Praise Ample Regions of Flesh"
"Vag on Vag: We Happy"

Marilyn Hacker

She says you are talking to a woman
disinteresting you and I wonder if
I am that woman disinteresting you
but think I disinterest not anyone
though being interesting assigns
problems when you are a woman
which you are not but I am a woman
interesting you are not talking to
and I ask, Why so disinterest yourself?
At Barnes and Noble (note 2 Barnes
1 Noble), a Chinese guy American
points to a white woman editorial
in the cafe and asks his friend if she
is the "chimp woman Jane Goodall"
cause she has "that Anglo patrician
look." I'll bet you have no bananas
there exist Anglo patrician men
disinterested in Goodall interesting
who (said particular patricians) spin
about their noggin a men's club of
mosquito netting or Pigpen's flotsam.
Once at a feminist writers' and so on,
I, needing more coffee, wondered
How do I ask Marilyn Hacker to move?
The woman was buttonholed in front
of the urn. I asked, How do you
ask Marilyn Hacker to move? She is
small and attentive and Marilyn Hacker.
My query disinteresting made her grin.

True Grit

I gave her backbone.
I told her, "You're a cool cat."

She said, "I wear my heart on my ankle,
And my head has burst into bloom."

"You have become a flesh-garden flower."
I did not warn her of the cold.

Or how the world will cut and encase
Until you wither.

You cannot dress up an ugly truth,
and a naked body does not need more.

Love Being Among Them

The only way two people
can make it work
(advise close consideration of
"work" "make" "it" and
seven other napkin holders)

is to inhabit a fearful present
beautiful in its
summation of so
times kicking
screaming (being how) thusly one
ends up an ivory
engraved and pouchy corpus

by which it is meant
not only to have now but
now be all and each skin pop
of retribution

to restart natural impulse aborted
when Babar & co.
were stole by lesser than gods
to neither pretend

Buffalo Springfield is on
the turntable nor
that even are "make" "it"
or "work" feasible

and so to arrive at the depot after
sitting in a car chicken-shit
packed (also feathers, old babies

venomous grandparents)
to expect no one knows you
are a soft kiss on
the sky at dawn, but
to discover same.

Like Wings

What can be said. Speed is
a calling. Desire is a bidding.

Judgment rises from steam
and then where?

Fortune is the heart of
two chambers like wings

and the instinct to soar,
survey the world and

its topographical gestures.
Topography is the back

of a woman seen as
desert or a reptile's spine,

rubbed to shattering
euphoria.

You have not learned to trust
(the muted instinct).

Risk is a crap shoot,
like prayer or begging.

You Are the Confusing Identity I Write For

You are the first line of this poem.
You are an opening gambit,
perplexity, a variable concept of relativity
space and time
in which this poem (you) exists.

This poem exists to be you, you, the woman I write for.
You're a man?
That's a wig? You are a man in a wig and, yes!
you are here! in this poem.
You are a conundrum and sparkling wine,
a Gewürztraminer or
cider with bubbles and no booze.

They say art enlightens.
Between you and me?
It might as well be a sleep mask.
Light rents space for its morning stretch.
This poem asked me to let out its seams.

You are the first and second lines of the final stanza and
you know why?
I'm hungry.
I'll always treasure our moments together.
Reader, if you were a seam, I'd take you out anywhere.

By Any

as if vertebrae slither in
and out of sensory cores,
her sideways glance is
an obligation you feel
in your skeletal skyscraper
I'll call the longing
spine, as if yoga masters
named it for, oh, what is
that word dragging you
on a walled-in carpet of
eels and alloys feet-first
to a couch long and soft
and oh, so wide, a couch
       so very wide.

Blame It on Family

She's a looker, linked to a rock,
struggling to sear fixed stories of
unreachable night into memory.

Stars shudder magnitudes
of flamboyance for a backatcha
to her pools of limp, liquid as Cassiopeia's
bedroom sighs.

Why is Andromeda chained?
Blame it on family.
Blame it all on family.

Perseus is a man modern with
gadgets–winged sandals,
flying horse, a Gorgon's severed head.
Like a man, he thinks he's part god.

This is a story of weight,
some from Gaea's rounded body,
a fly-over for Perseus returning Andromeda
to Ethiopia or Palestine, depending who's telling.

Andromeda longs to be in
heaven's fearless ice, knowing it's beautiful
to be brave and in chains.

The Quiet Softness

About Queen Dido, you wonder,
if at some point early enough for
self-prevention she could have
hung up mythology for a safe
nakedness of, hey, herself, even
if judged (when the world sees you
as you were born it confronts fear
of isolation and transformation,
and the world detests confrontation
unless it's brutal and there's victory
or a shield or rhymed manuscript
rendering titanic loss as fame).
Dido was Phoenician. I would like
to be Phoenician, say it with me,
Phoenician. Don't you like me
more, now? Forgetting rapture in
the arms of an accomplished heart
or the quiet softness of a penis
sighing, Aeneas sailed his cock
to Rome, leaving her in Carthage,
the city of her breasts stomach
hips, configurations of the universe.
Dido. Were his promises to be
believed, really. You can still
tell him no. And it's going to be
a while before translations of war
and abandonment no longer make
sense. In your lovely city you can
weep. Yours, you built it, weep.

It Was the Year the Birds Held a Conference

It was the year we wove vests of night-blooming
jasmine. We wore them lightly.
Our breasts fell in love.

It was the year enchantments sold
two-for-one or five for a blessing.
Our pillows filled with grasshoppers.
Crickets deciphered our dreams.

That year children became pinwheels.
That year Ferris wheels spun out-of-control.

It was the year birds held a conference.
At scheduled breaks they perched on our
shoulders, singing songs of love and loss.
After a rain the land wept at the beauty of life.

Keeping It Holy

Vickie told the story about
going out for a carton of milk
on Christmas Day, and
all the stores being closed and
her feeling sly for thinking of Fairfax Ave.,
where David's stars lived.
Stars because they made it out.
Because slow stellar disintegration
no longer serves as model for
astrophysicists and the observant.
Stars because they were alive,
these men and women in black suits
tailored for vaudeville, in
skirts forced to fall like Adam
and Eve to a punishing length.
It's a thing, for mystics to see
the unknown in valleys and
hills, children and parents,
in leaves dry winds scatter.
No coffee, and I am a cardboard
stand-in for an empty storefront,
all Potemkin, so I am pro-Vickie.
That year, Christmas fell on Saturday,
the Sabbath, when stores close
so whomever-cannot-be-named
may sit back and do nothing,
at which divinity excels, take
the religious wars of Europe,
millions of brand and off-brand
believers slaughtered in the name of.
Yet to the Vickie went the milk,
finally, at a 7-Eleven on Sunset.
And the coffee was filled with joy.

No One Asks

Did Jesus Christ love himself?
Jesus who spent all of
forty days and forty nights
where pilgrims and the Prophet,
praise his name, prayed?

Jesus who saw god, the
one, the mountain burning,
the desert wandering,
the god who must transform
for the world to.

We all resist temptation.
We'd all be happy or
dead if we didn't.

(Mom died, a blessing.
She was eighty-six and
willful like us.)

Mary prays when there's
an amber alert.
I touch her foot to conquer
a polychrome snake's
faded slither.

Early Jazz

Like most artists,
Johann Sebastian Bach
moved to the city.

Sometimes you need
a point of entrance for
ornamental notes and flourishes.

So a crazy organist
can staff the future with
musicians who rest, yeah,
but mainly soar.

Drink, Child

I asked for the water.
Reverend Mother ladled liquid enough
I wished I'd brought conditioner.
Soft is the message of the Lord.

Does Jesus Christ love moms who inhabit
faith like a body of track-marks inhabits a
T-shirt washed thin, stretched on skin so lean
a glance from Caesar draws blood?

Come, you mighty clouds,
mystery accumulated by explanation.
To end sufferings, women, mothers
      drunk or gone
      sexing or gone
we need, what do I say here, we need
not go gentle just be it.

From between their legs, children fall off
a table, bags of oranges
      chocked with Vitamin C
      and dented.

Watch the magus
unpack her heart in the heat of Arabian sun.
Spot the magus
lifting her hearts in the heat of Arabian sun.

Oh fat-breasted goddess
fat-bellied goddess
born in Africa before all birth,
three sacred rivers flow
from your throat
in blues sequenced to heal.

Not Simple Is Joy nor Cosmology

She has so little understanding of
anything she should have some
understanding of—night's dragon-star
breath so hot, no one feels safe or wants to.

Flames, flares, torches and still
night begs for warmth.

We are without enough cover or
with too much—what does she know—
to keep our caravan safe.

In her understanding of things,
stars are whistling-sharp.
She won't believe she is on a planet.
I tell her but she hasn't seen proof.

She can prove she is on a bed on a floor
suspended over lives tender and arrogant.
Anything else?

Tenderness isn't necessary but there it is
like a chemical we write Congress about.
Which gets into our system.

Arrogance isn't there, it's here,
the battle, opposing sides, arms.
The erotic a spy who gives up secrets—
but never all.

Night is reluctant to leave.
Have you noticed?
It too is afraid of stars and
at dawn cries out for relief, for mercy.

I was led to pray for mercy once.
Now I pray in a general sort of way.
If Whoever Shaped Stars shaped stars
She wants *us*—me and you—
to gather them, not to reach Her, but
to find each other—do you understand?

A Scarlet Moss

It was weird. Mom disapproved and
Pop started shaking like he'd
seen a fluffy pooch.
He has his fears.
I stripped.
So what if I'm blubbery?
I want to roll on whorish moss.
I could wake up or you could set fire to
the marriage counselor.
Love so slippery needs handles.
Wedding planners are a food group.
So is roast beef.
The horseradish of a different color is pink.
I hope a scarlet moss covers the land.
All I'll need is

rub its space fiction with bare feet.
The human soul has been invaded.
Rub it and heal.

And the Ships Set Off

In the desert where God grew a goddess, a snake, a devil, temptation and time to think I found a clay pot containing knowledge of more than me. The clay pot wasn't for sale so I stole it. The world is worth a broken tablet. In the clay pot containing knowledge of more than me wars were swapped and elegies of them. Used-up gods were tricked-out as luck, good, bad and to be determined. There was dancing and indigestion. The punch packed a wallop. Snakes bid for attention. What they hissed was anyone's guess. Oh. There was Helen. Knowledge of greater than me is a universal. Knowledge of the specific of me is a boutique. Knowledge of Helen and me is yours for the asking. She was a keeper, was kept and I, like another, stole her to keep her. A woman like that for a woman like me is worth a broken tablet.

Please Don't Think I'm Being Disrespectful

The church was hot. I drank holy water.
Just like that I was Jesus at the well.

Lower the bucket into a caged spring.
Your skin holds together but how together are you?
Our flaw is sunk deeper than a well.

I asked a Samaritan woman for help.
Now I am the Samaritan woman and
      you are he.

Story is best friend and long-found love.
Don't lead a dress pattern life,
      a bed-in-a-bag life.

He who was thirsty and also a prime number
told the Samaritan who was a woman,
      The One is spirit.

From my two semesters of Homeric Greek:
"psyche" translates as spirit and soul and breath,
      as in *The goddess has bad breath.*

Not to mention her spirit and soul.

Time Lives to Thwart Chronology

It's the same in dreams as in life.
We're trying to figure it out
and missing the finish line
of blinking fireflies punching
our names into velvet sky.
So many ways to spell poet
—"fool"—"layabout"—
"competitor." We must proofread.

Attention being equal to blue cheese,
you being equal to a bag of greens
a drizzle of olive oil
sliced antioxidants,
distraction equal to
a turnip driving a gray Mercedes
crumbled over the works.

Mindfulness is ready as
second-rate parchment or
certain cheeses to shatter.

Life's an actor rushing to the stage,
breathless but on book.
God is Walt Whitman on Mickle Street
liking the wealthy well as
those we're asked to remember
(the lonely)
in our supplications.

Screw the human condition.

There are moments we're satisfied with
the timidity and injustice.
We've breathed hard times—
hard times! we say.

A little punishment of someone else
could make us feel good—
for a moment—and—clear to me—
it's important we feel good.

Saint Beauty

In the direct way of the foolish,
St. Francis walked up to a wolf
and said *Brother*.

It was a generic naming
with Gubbio's villagers murmuring
    mashed potatoes
    mashed potatoes
like actors creating scrim in
a Perry Mason juror's box.

This was not the wolf who dressed
in Granny's flannel gown and tied on
a nightcap. No, this was Brother Wolf
touching paw to palm:
    I'll be good.

What's to learn from this story?
Feed all creatures until
claimed from Lost & Found?

Goodness is a gamble.
Perry proved beauty is no defense.
The mystery of being is
trumped by the mystery of not-being.

Flesh needs flesh,
even that grandmother's,
toasty in her long flannel gown.

Call Me Sheena

Easier to make an enemy than beef Wellington.
An ill wind blows "Mandy."
No one can hear you sing "Polly Wolly Doodle" in space.
Oedipus is Supideo backwards.
Call me Sheena.
When you die no one can hear you slurp.
The Liberal Arts are no substitute for a hot bath.
Lemon pepper has come and gone.
As ye sow so shall ye perform a triple axel.
Mint jelly will pinch-hit for sixth-period history.
Your anger turned to tapioca.
Your toes turned in.
That's not your bra, is it?
The guns of August are summering.
Inconsolable angels go shopping.
Satan covered the casserole with grated Cheddar.
A mist covered the sports desk.
The willow grabbed for designer Kleenex.
All good things must bend.
Sing glory for the Lord She is great.
Sing glory for the Host serves good snacks.

Inquisition

We boiled the eggs until they confessed their sins
so many and devilish although how trembling
raw yolk could see so far into its hardening future
as to delineate transgressions we cannot explain
but suggest our effervescented two acceded to
leading interrogation as they scrambled to be free.
We cannot be bothered with intricacy of huevo
or humanity. We must have our meal. We must live.

So Tender Beauty

A sign of your times, a rose-happy glow
enameled on dawn's fingertips, a smiling
hardhat Phoebus harnessing wild geldings
to a mythic time-oiled chariot for another
day's work. You don't think the sun just
hangs around? Illumination rolls in place
for your enlightenment. Spirits assess
your purpose on the planet. No abyss
with you falling falling hurtling big,
and yet you're loath to enter atmospheres
of the day. You and oblong room cuddle
in swirled string-thin beams swaying like
genetic tinsel draping lofting evergreens.
At tables in your room of living, huffing
scalding coffee perked, their coffee cups
clinking in your room of life, a charmed
crew. And saucers with tendril and fleur.
Square-napkins-mere sop spills that are just
gonna happen in your room of life in your
life eternal as it courtly bops you to
extravagant nows infused by murderous
urges briefly just. The best become
expansive. In a spray of silvered light
a butterfly boasting so tender beauty, we
forgive its disaffirmation of the cocoon.

An Interrogatory

Nothing but smooth sailing.
           Isley Brothers

Those aren't birds are they are they,
are they?, or are they insects of an ilk

glowing and hovering hummingbird-
like though not hummingbird, not bird,

no, I see it, that which I wasn't seeing,
a lingering phosphorescence, no

luminescence, oh!, it is incandescence
and those are seraphim I see, I am

seeing seraphim, six-winged seraphim,
seraphim having six wings or so said

Isaiah, a seraphim seer, two wings, fans
over a mighty face, two enfolding feet

and two neon wings to lift them aloft,
smoothly sail above prophesies for our

tangled times, two wings golden as honey
is gold, as amber is gold, as transparency

is gold, carry us to a feared eternal now,
tolerable, almost, when we sing along.

The Risen Barbie

i.
If Rapunzel had a bob
If the prince were less charming
If the witch a vegetarian
If the carousel had legs

ii.
The Beatitudes Barbie
The Leper Barbie
The Dead Lazarus Barbie
The Risen Barbie
Barbie at the Well

iii.
If Hendrix
If Buddy
If Richie
If Kurt
Jim, Amy, Otis, Janis.
Nick, Sid, Tupac
The Notorious B.I.G.

iv.
If Death is real
If the Divine goes
shopping for a MacBook Air
If we achieve Paradise
If the cool kids snub us
(Ah, but the wonderful witty
Welcome, wherever we go)

White Tunnel and the Night Return

I was vessel, dumb animal receptor.
DNA snaked me into life,
three insurrectionist rivers carried me.
Antiquity was my patron saint.

I heard a call before I heard a call,
an off-rhythm more fluid than any
legacy code patriarchal in my cells.
A woman floating, I splashed
oceanic palms my sisters envied,
light-years off. I have been lucky.

Jesus, dance with me.
Mary, in your arms.

No one said anything, let alone,
It will be easy.
The writers said, It will be hard,
ethics and a capacity for reason and doubt,
a daily crucifixion.
The shills asked for Barabbas.
Every freakin' day. *Barabbas!*

Jesus, dance with me.
Mary, in your arms.

Just now I prayed the Kindness
funnel herself to this subway car.
I am wet clay, not the wind.
I can't part seas of red, infirmity
from body, rage from the raging.

Dance with me, Jesus.
Hold me, Mary.

You must have the strength of
Ozymandias and consider his stupidity,
a "heart that feeds"—a "hand that mocks."

There is nothing out of place, Jesus.
Hold me, Mary. I might be wrong.

From Love, Imagination

As many bridges as I can walk
I have, suspended over

water's bounded body,
a bent-limb river flowing

in imitation of life's farewells.
Over opaline bowls and

chipped basins where nets
are cast so fathers and sons

can feed the hungry and
holy daughters work mysteries

of bounty: We are flesh and
gifted sustenance.

Along a roadbed I lose myself in
elemental apocalypse,

earth water air—and fire rushing
over the rumble spilling from

a reedy source to
a greater body demanding tribute.

Far on the Lake, Watery Lake

They stole a boat   an
old floating shoe box
with choices   one of which
was *I won't sink* and it   didn't.
   Good thing. They had
a place to go to   lay low in
   tug toward   a hideout.

Big   the lake   its blue
an historical   smudge of
remorse and   archangel.
   That meant something.
Passports were passed
   ported   stamped silly.

They had a place to go
   the going necessitated by
acts that were   wrong
or weren't or they   did do
   or didn't   but once the
thinking was thought
   they might as well have.

She used a color stick
the color of   leaves-turning-
hair into forested   fire.
Asked   *Should we take
out   the trash?*
   To fool trackers. They did.

A mountain pass from   child-
hood to the freeing squalor
  appeared as a fog   lifted
  itself   accepted itself for

     what it was or wasn't
     without knowing

Its thirst
     for mystery   fueled
          the long ride.

Notes

"Thank the Cashier": Emily Post quotation is from *Etiquette in Society, in Business, in Politics and at Home* on Bartleby.com

"Love Being Among Them": is from a line in "The Second" (*Elephant Rocks*) by Kay Ryan.

"Not Just to Amuse": "not just to amuse" and "assenting angels" are from the tenth of Rainier Maria Rilke's *Duino Elegies*. Translator A.S. Kline, 2001; offered online by the translator.

"It Was the Year the Birds Held a Conference." From Joanna Fuhrman's *The Year of Yellow Butterflies* blog. (Hanging Loose Press).

"The Risen Barbie": Jimi Hendrix, Buddy Holly, Richie Valens, Kurt Cobain, Jim Morrison, Amy Winehouse, Otis Redding, Janis Joplin, Nick Drake, Sid Vicious, Tupac Shakur, The Notorious B.I.G.

"This Way and That": "It was a fairy funeral." William Blake's contemporary Allan Cunningham wrote of Blake's vision. In *The Life of Blake* by Alexander Gilchrist (1863) (Google books).

Acknowledgments

I extend much gratitude to the following editors, publishers, and journals:

Barrow Street: The Short Lapse of It; So Let's See if I Have this Right
Before Passing (Great weather for MEDIA): Swept Away
Berfrois: The Avoirdupois Chic
Bone Bouquet: Far on the Lake, Watery Lake
Boston Review: From Love, Imagination; So Tender Beauty
Cordite Poetry Journal: Fabian Avenarius (Arthur Craven)
EOAGH: Inquisition; One Day a Year You Can Take Something Home from the Met
Fairy Tale Review: Anxieties
Folly Magazine: Drink, Child
Geographies of Soul and Taffeta (Indolent Books): Family; Interrogatory
Golden Walkman: Who punched the banana!
Gone Lawn: Complexities Run Interference.
ISACOUSTIC: No One Asks
Lavender Review: This Way and That; Longing for a Blue Sky
Like a Fat Gold Watch: Meditations on Sylvia Plath & Living (FGW Press): Not Simple Is Joy Nor Cosmology
Maintenant 6: Pasted and Cut
Mary: A Literary Quarterly: White People Are on My Mind
MiPoesias: A Scarlet Moss
No, Dear: Motherhood
Oddball Magazine: Corpses and Cats
Painted Bride Quarterly: Popularity
Parthenon West: Hockney at Bellevue
POOL: You Are the Confusing Identity I Write For

Posit: White Tunnel and the Night Return
Prelude: This Once-in-a-Lifetime Opportunity; Please Don't Think I'm Being Disrespectful; Wish Me Luck
Redheaded Stepchild: After the Plague Years; Blame It on Family
Sinister Wisdom: Hatred Is a Death Threat; On the Shelving Cart
St. Katherine's Review: Legend with Usual Cruelties
SWWIM: After the Greeks Tippy-toed Out of a Horse
The Wallace Stevens Journal: Early Jazz
The Writing Disorder: When a Heated Gazebo Must Do
Thrush: Time Passes and Fails
Vending Machine Press: Science and Change; By Any; And the Ships Set Off; The Reversible Lobotomy of Confusion; Six Aunts Wobbling
West Wind Review: Call Me Sheena; Marilyn Hacker

About the Author

Sarah Sarai is a writer and independent editor. Her first poetry collection, *The Future Is Happy* BlazeVOX[books], was: "A labyrinth. Walt Whitman. Sméagol with his ring in his pocket. Holden Caulfield. Humbert Humbert. Jane Eyre. Mecca. The Zig Zag Man" (Stephen Page). Her most recent chapbook, *Geographies of Soul and Taffeta* (Indolent Books), was: "fierce and inventive" (Mary Meriam). Sarah has an MFA from Sarah Lawrence College. *That Strapless Bra in Heaven* is her second full-length poetry collection. She is a Californian living in New York City.

www.ingramcontent.com/pod-product-compliance
Lightning Source LLC
LaVergne TN
LVHW091318080426
835510LV00007B/544